DINOSAUR ENCYCLOPEDIA FOR KIDS

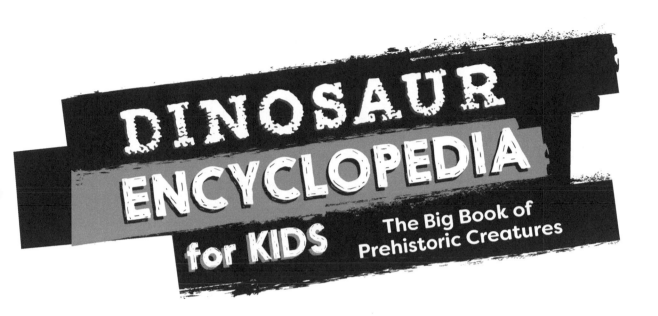

DINOSAUR ENCYCLOPEDIA for KIDS

The Big Book of Prehistoric Creatures

"Dinosaur George" Blasing
and Cary Woodruff

Illustrations by Annalisa and Marina Durante

ROCKRIDGE
PRESS

Interior and Cover Designer: Francesca Pacchini
Art Producer: Tom Hood
Editor: Alyson Penn
Production Editor: Nora Milman
Production Manager: Martin Worthington

Illustrations © Annalisa and Marina Durante, 2021. Author photograph courtesy of Jack Wilson. Illustrators' photograph courtesy of Fredi Marcarini.

Hardcover ISBN: 978-1-63878-634-4 | Paperback ISBN: 978-1-63807-384-0 | eBook ISBN: 978-1-63878-020-5
R0

CONTENTS

INTRODUCTION

WHAT IS A DINOSAUR?

Dinosaurs are some of the most amazing animals that ever lived. These fascinating creatures make our imaginations run wild. They could be as tall as a four-story building, or as small as a chicken. Some had spectacular spikes or scales, whereas others had **frills** or even feathers. With their huge teeth and razor-sharp claws, some dinosaurs were fierce hunters that ate other animals—even other dinosaurs.

Dinosaurs are a group of reptiles that first lived about 245 million years ago. They all share a common ancestor. This group, or clade, is called Dinosauria. The earliest-known dinosaurs were small, two-legged, and hunted for food. Over time, they **evolved** to have a wide range of body sizes and diets.

This book is filled with fun facts that show you how different dinosaurs lived and what they looked like. When you see a tricky term in **bold**, turn to the glossary at the back of the book to learn its definition and dig up more dino knowledge. Are you ready to travel back in time to the Age of Dinosaurs? Let's go!

PREHISTORIC TIME

Did you know that not all dinosaurs lived at the same time? The first dinosaurs lived about 245 million years ago, but most dinosaurs lived during the Mesozoic Era. This era is divided into three time periods: Triassic, Jurassic, and Cretaceous. Different dinosaurs lived in each one.

TRIASSIC PERIOD

This period is when dinosaurs first lived on Earth. It began 251 million years ago and lasted until 201 million years ago.

JURASSIC PERIOD

From 201 to 145 million years ago. This period is sometimes called the "Age of Giants" because some of the largest dinosaurs, known as **sauropods**, grew to huge sizes during this time.

TRIASSIC   JURASSIC   CRETACEOUS

MESOZOIC ERA

CRETACEOUS PERIOD

From 145 to 66 million years ago. Some of the most well-known dinosaurs, such as *Velociraptor*, *Triceratops*, and *Tyrannosaurus rex*, lived during this time period.

CENOZOIC ERA

From 66 million years ago through today. This period is also known as the "Age of Mammals."

PALEOCENE EOCENE OLIGOCENE MIOCENE PLIOCENE PLEISTOCENE HOLOCENE

CENOZOIC ERA

UNDERWATER CREATURES

Before animals could walk on land, they swam. In fact, the first animals on Earth lived in the water. A very long time ago, the seas were filled with swimming **prehistoric** creatures. We learn everything that we know about prehistoric creatures from **fossils**.

Paleontologists are the scientists who dig up and study the fossils of plants and animals. Thanks to fossils, we know which prehistoric animals could swim, what they ate, and how long ago they lived. Some swimming creatures, like fish and sharks, lived 300 million years before dinosaurs ever appeared!

The **evolution** of arms began with the fins of a fish. These fins were made of one large bone that connected to two smaller bones, just like your arms! Those bones then connected to many tiny bones, like your fingers.

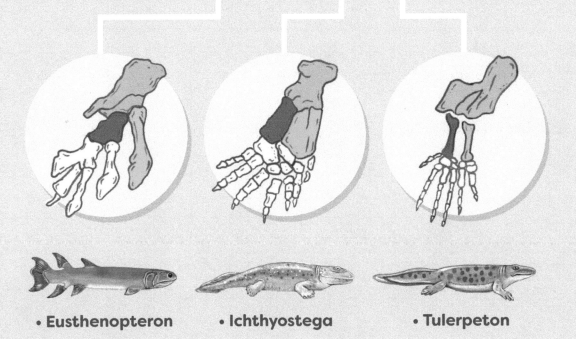

MILLIONS OF YEARS AGO

420   400   380   360

• Eusthenopteron   • Ichthyostega   • Tulerpeton

CARNIVORES

A **carnivore** is an animal that eats only meat. Carnivorous dinosaurs are called **theropods**. Paleontologists can tell what a dinosaur ate by the shape of its teeth and claws. Sharp, pointy teeth could cut into meat. Sharp, curved claws could grip and hold **prey**. There were many different kinds of theropods. The smallest was the size of a chicken, and the largest was as long as an 18-wheeler truck. Theropods like *Tyrannosaurus rex* were tall enough to look through an upstairs window of a two-story house!

Theropods may seem scary, but these meat-eating dinosaurs were not evil. They played an important role.

 Without carnivores, there would have been too many plant eaters. By hunting plant-eating animals, carnivores helped protect plants and keep the balance of life on Earth.

WHAT IS BRONTOSAURUS?

The *Brontosaurus* was a giant sauropod that lived during the Jurassic Period. This herbivore had a long, thin neck and a long tail like a whip. The name *Brontosaurus* means "thunder lizard," but that wasn't always this dinosaur's name. In 1877, a famous paleontologist discovered part of a giant sauropod skeleton. He named it *Apatosaurus ajax*. Later, in 1879, he found a similar but larger skeleton. He named this one *Brontosaurus excelsus*. Paleontologists were confused. Were they really two different dinosaurs? The *Apatosaurus* skeleton was of a younger dinosaur, so they thought it might be the same as the *Brontosaurus*. They changed both names to *Apatosaurus*, but everyone liked the name of *Brontosaurus* better. In 2015, paleontologists found that *Brontosaurus* was different enough to be its own dinosaur again.

HERBIVORES

An **herbivore** is an animal that eats only plants. Herbivores had special teeth made for slicing or chewing plants. The smallest herbivore dinosaur was the size of a house cat, and the largest was longer than four school buses parked in a row. Some long-necked dinosaurs were tall enough to look through the highest window of a six-story building!

Of the 700 known dinosaur **species**, 560 were herbivores. To help organize so many kinds of herbivores, paleontologists created different family groups.

Sauropodomorphs: Long-necked plant eaters that included the biggest of all dinosaurs, the sauropods.

Ankylosaurs: These dinosaurs had body **armor**, and some had a club at the end of their tail.

Ceratopsians: They had horns and frills on their heads.

Stegosaurs: Many had plates on their back and spikes on their tail.

Ornithopods: They had birdlike feet and beaks. Some even had duck-like bills. The smaller ones walked on hind legs.

Pachycephalosaurs: Known as "boneheads," they had thick skulls.

Herbivore dinosaurs ate a variety of plants, from **conifer** and pine needles to ferns and bushes. Some traveled in herds, and others lived alone. Each had different ways of defending themselves against carnivores. Plant-eating dinosaurs were very important to the **ecosystem** because they ate the seeds of plants and then spread them to new areas. They also kept the land from becoming overgrown.

FLYING CREATURES

Some prehistoric flying creatures were dinosaurs. Other creatures, like **pterosaurs**, flew above the heads of early dinosaurs. Pterosaurs were flying reptiles that lived at the same time as dinosaurs. Although they looked like dinosaurs, they belonged to a different family.

How do paleontologists know that dinosaurs and pterosaurs are different? Because all dinosaurs have a big hole in their hip socket and a large **crest** on their upper arm bone, and pterosaurs don't. Birds evolved from small, meat-eating dinosaurs that walked the land and survive to this day.

Hummingbird, ostrich, pigeon, eagle, penguin, peacock, chicken—every single bird you know is a living dinosaur!

Chicken skeleton   *Dinosaur skeleton*

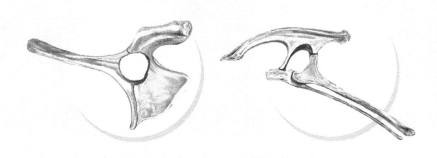

Pterosaur hip bone   *Dinosaur hip bone*

On the dinosaur family tree, dinosaurs and pterosaurs are like cousins.

WHAT HAPPENED TO THE DINOSAURS?

Dinosaurs existed for 177 million years until an enormous **asteroid** struck Earth. The impact was so big that it created a huge dust cloud. This cloud blocked the sunlight for almost a year. It caused plants and the animals that depended on light and sun, like the dinosaurs, to become **extinct**. This event that happened 66 million years ago is known as the Cretaceous-Paleogene extinction. It marked the end of the Mesozoic Era.

Fortunately, one group of dinosaurs survived the extinction: birds! Dinosaurs still exist in the form of birds and there are more than 10,000 species of birds living today in our Cenozoic Era.

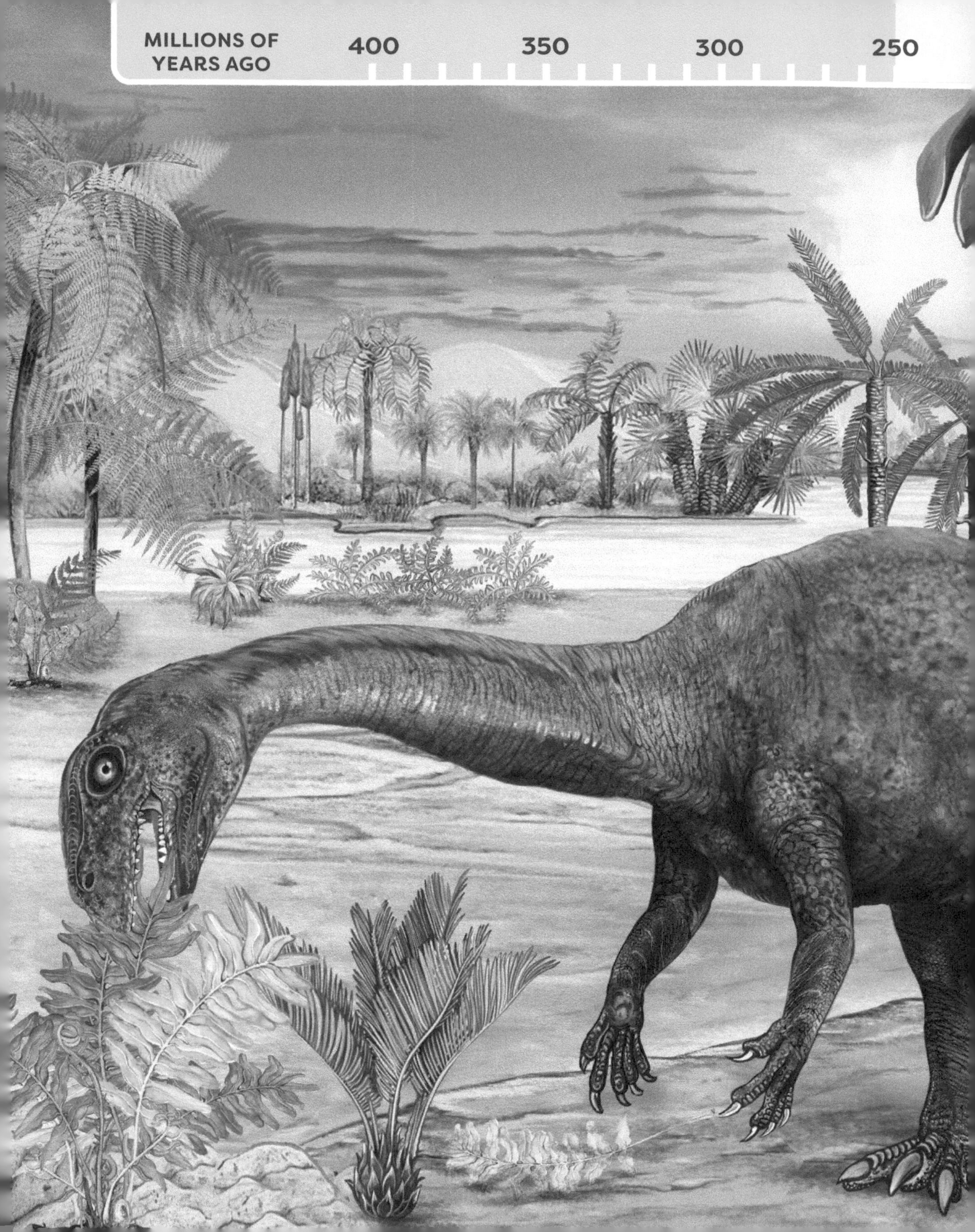
MILLIONS OF YEARS AGO
400
350
300
250

PART ONE

TRIASSIC PERIOD

The Triassic Period marks the beginning of the Mesozoic Era. It began 251 million years ago and lasted until 201 million years ago. This is when dinosaurs first lived on Earth. They evolved with many other animals during this time, living in the sea, on the land, and soaring in the air.

Atopodentatus means "strange tooth" because of its odd teeth and the shape of its snout.

ATOPODENTATUS

SAY IT! ah-TOP-oh-DEN-ta-tuss

Atopodentatus had a snout shaped like a vacuum cleaner. This wide snout helped it graze and feed on tiny algae on the sea floor. Almost all other **marine** reptiles are **predators** that eat fish, squid, or even one another. Scientists know of only two marine reptiles that did not eat meat. *Atopodentatus* was perhaps one of the very first marine reptiles that was an herbivore.

The first *Atopodentatus* fossil ever found was damaged. This made paleontologists think that *Atopodentatus* could open its mouth to the left and right, in addition to up and down!

Length: almost 10 feet

When: Middle Triassic period—245 to 228 million years ago

Where: China

It ate: algae

It was the size of: a lion

SHASTASAURUS

SAY IT! SHAZ-tah-SORE-us

Shastasaurus is the largest marine reptile ever discovered! Just like whale sharks that swim in the ocean today, *Shastasaurus* was a gentle giant. *Shastasaurus* swam slowly, powered by four large paddles. It had a short snout and no teeth, which means that it probably swallowed its prey whole.

Shastasaurus means "Mount Shasta lizard" because the first fossil was found near Mount Shasta in California, USA.

Length: up to 70 feet

When: Middle to Late Triassic period—235 to 205 million years ago

Where: North America and China

It ate: squid

It was the size of: an oak tree

You can see a nearly complete skeleton of *Shastasaurus* at the Royal Tyrell Museum in Alberta, Canada.

Henodus is the only placodont that's been found in fresh water.

HENODUS

SAY IT! hen-NO-duss

With its arms, legs, tail, and head coming out of a shell, you may think that *Henodus* was a turtle. But it was not! *Henodus* looks like a turtle because of **convergent evolution**. The two creatures both have shells to protect them from predators. But the shell of *Henodus* and a turtle's shell are very different. On a turtle, most of the shell is made from the turtle's rib bones. But on *Henodus*, the shell is made of many pieces of bone that stick to the outside of its skeleton. The pieces fit together like a puzzle.

Henodus belonged to a group of marine reptiles with flat, box-shaped teeth called the placodonts. Placodontia means "tablet teeth."

Length: 3 feet

When: Late Triassic period—228 to 220 million years ago

Where: Germany

It ate: aquatic plants

It was the size of: a large dog

HERRERASAURUS

SAY IT! Huh-RARE-uh-SAWR-us

EORAPTOR

SAY IT! EE-oh-RAP-tur

Length: 13 feet	**Length:** 3 feet
Height: 5.5 feet	**Height:** 2 feet
Weight: 700 pounds	**Weight:** 20 pounds
When: Late Triassic period—228 to 216 million years ago	**When:** Late Triassic period—228 to 216 million years ago
Where: the forests of Argentina	**Where:** the forests of Argentina
It ate: *Eoraptor* and large reptiles	**It ate:** insects, fish, lizards, and eggs
It was the size of: a lion	**It was the size of:** a turkey

During the Late Triassic Period, *Herrerasaurus* was the largest meat-eating dinosaur on Earth! This big predator could take on almost any prey, including the *Eoraptor*. *Eoraptor* was a smaller predator but fast hunter. It may have hunted at night so it could sneak up on prey. It also used the darkness to hide from *Herrerasaurus*.

Herrerasaurus had five toes but only walked on three. *Eoraptor* had five fingers.

Herrerasaurus had a flexible joint in its lower jaw that let it slide back and forth.

Eoraptor had claws that helped it run on sand, mud, or hard ground.

COELOPHYSIS

SAY IT! See-low-FY-sis

Paleontologists know a lot about *Coelophysis* because dozens of skeletons were found in a place called Ghost Ranch in New Mexico, USA. This "dinosaur **graveyard**" was created when a large **pack** of *Coelophysis* were crossing a flooded stream. Adults and babies were found at this site, proving that these dinosaurs lived in family groups. One skeleton had the bones of a baby crocodile in its stomach—its last meal!

It was the fastest animal in its environment.

Length: 10 feet

Height: 3 feet

Weight: 40 pounds

When: Late Triassic/ Early Jurassic period—228 to 196 million years ago

Where: the forests of Arizona and New Mexico in the United States, and possibly Africa

It ate: insects, fish, reptiles, and eggs

It was the size of: a great white shark

RIOJASAURUS

SAY IT! ree-OH-ha-SAWR-us

Riojasaurus was an early sauropodomorph that may have been related to the great sauropods. Like its later cousins, it had a long neck and whiplike tail. At first, some paleontologists believed that *Riojasaurus* could only stand on four feet. But new studies show that it could stand, walk, and even run on its back legs. This also allowed it to reach higher into trees.

Length: 33 feet

Height: 7 feet

Weight: 7,000 pounds

When: Late Triassic period—216 to 203 million years

Where: the forests of Argentina

It ate: plants

It was the size of: a small school bus

Riojasaurus had thick skin that protected it during attack.

It had very large claws on its hands that could be used for defense.

It may have been able to drink over 20 gallons of water a day.

PLATEOSAURUS

SAY IT! PLAT-ee-oh-SAWR-us

Plateosaurus was probably the largest, heaviest dinosaur on Earth at the time. It had special teeth that could chew through the toughest **vegetation**. This means that *Plateosaurus* could eat many different kinds of plants. It walked on four legs, but it could also stand up on its two rear legs. This helped when it wanted to reach high into trees. *Plateosaurus* had long claws on each hand. They could be used to grab branches or defend against predators.

Plateosaurus may have lived to be 20 years old.

Length: 26 feet

Height: 12 feet

Weight: 8,000 pounds

When: Late Triassic period—214 to 204 million years ago

Where: the forests of South Africa

It ate: plants

It was the size of: a large truck

MUSSAURUS

SAY IT! moos-SAWR-us

Mussaurus was one of the first sauropodomorph dinosaurs that ever lived. Its name means "mouse lizard" because the first skeleton found was very small. Later discoveries proved that this **specimen** was just a baby. Paleontologists have also found *Mussaurus* eggs. The babies likely lived with their mother until they were old enough to protect themselves from predators. *Mussaurus* was probably fast and relied on speed to escape attack.

A baby *Mussaurus* could fit in your palm.

It had five fingers on each hand.

Length: 20 feet

Height: 6 feet

Weight: 2,000 pounds

When: Late Triassic period—214 to 203 million years ago

Where: the forests of Argentina

It ate: plants

It was the size of: a pickup truck

Caelestiventus is the earliest-known desert-dwelling pterosaur.

Copies of *Caelestiventus* bones have been 3D printed!

CAELESTIVENTUS

SAY IT! Say-LESS-tah-VIN-tuss

Other pterosaurs lived in forests or near water, but *Caelestiventus* lived in the desert. It had over 100 pointy teeth that it probably used to eat small animals. Because pterosaur bones are thin and delicate, they often get squished during **fossilization**. *Caelestiventus* is a special fossil because many of its parts were not squished. To study these fragile bones, scientists scanned the rocks at a hospital to examine them on a computer.

Wingspan: 5 feet

When: Late Triassic period—208 million years ago

Where: Western United States

It ate: perhaps insects and small reptiles. Paleontologists don't know.

It was the size of: a cat

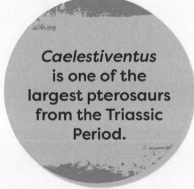

Caelestiventus is one of the largest pterosaurs from the Triassic Period.

PART TWO

JURASSIC PERIOD

After the Triassic Period came the Jurassic Period. This period lasted from 201 million to 145 million years ago. During this time, the largest dinosaurs grew to huge sizes. Earth was rich with vegetation and food, which might be why they evolved large bodies.

Dilophosaurus may have used its tail to swim!

DILOPHOSAURUS

SAY IT! Dye-LOAF-oh-SAWR-us

Dilophosaurus had two crests that ran along the top of its skull from its nose to its eyes. It had thin, light bones and arms that couldn't move much. That meant this carnivore used its jaws and teeth to catch prey like fish and small animals.

Length: 23 feet

Height: 5 feet

Weight: 880 pounds

When: Early Jurassic period—199 to 189 million years ago

Where: the forests of Arizona in the United States

It ate: fish, baby crocodiles, and small plant-eating dinosaurs

It was the size of: an SUV

Its upper teeth were almost twice as long as its lower teeth.

A strange hook on its upper jaw may have helped hold slippery prey like fish.

CRYOLOPHOSAURUS

SAY IT! Cry-oh-LOAF-oh-SAWR-us

Cryolophosaurus means "frozen crested reptile." This carnivore was discovered in Antarctica. Although it is cold and frozen today, parts of Antarctica were warmer and covered in forests during the Age of Dinosaurs. *Cryolophosaurus* had a crest on its head. Scientists aren't sure what it was used for, but it was thin and fragile, so they know it wasn't used for battle. *Cryolophosaurus* was the top predator in its area.

Cryolophosaurus was one of the largest predators on Earth during the time it lived.

Length: 20 feet

Height: 7 feet

Weight: 1,000 pounds

When: Early Jurassic period—189 to 183 million years ago

Where: the forests of Antarctica

It ate: small mammals, flying reptiles, and young sauropods

It was the size of: a truck

MEGALOSAURUS

SAY IT! MEG-uh-low-SAWR-us

Megalosaurus was the first dinosaur to ever receive a name. Scientists named it in 1824. The name means "big reptile." At first, scientists thought *Megalosaurus* walked on four legs like a lizard or crocodile. But after more study, they discovered that it walked on its back legs. This dinosaur was a large, strong carnivore that could take on almost anything that lived in its **territory**.

Megalosaurus may have scratched trees to keep its claws sharp, just like bears and cats do today.

Megalosaurus could catch its own food or steal the meals of smaller meat eaters.

Length: 30 feet

Height: 10 feet

Weight: 4,500 pounds

When: Middle Jurassic period—175 to 155 million years ago

Where: the forests and shores of England

It ate: medium and large plant-eating dinosaurs

It was the size of: a school bus

MONOLOPHOSAURUS

SAY IT! MON-uh-LOAF-oh-SAWR-us

Monolophosaurus means "single-crested lizard." It was named for the large, hollow crest on the top of its skull. Some scientists think the crest helped with its sense of smell. Others think they used it to attract a **mate** or threaten a rival. This medium-size predator most likely hid in trees and bushes until a plant-eating dinosaur walked by. Then it could pounce on its prey!

Its stiff tail helped it change directions quickly when running at top speed.

Length: 16.5 feet

Height: 4 feet tall

Weight: 1,000 pounds

When: Middle Jurassic period—167 to 161 million years ago

Where: the forests of China

It ate: lizards, fish, and small and medium dinosaurs

It was the size of: a whale

Leedsichthys was the largest fish with a bony skeleton.

LEEDSICHTHYS

SAY IT! LEADS-ick-these

Leedsichthys was a very large fish, but it wasn't a scary predator. It was actually very gentle. As it swam through the ocean, *Leedsichthys* kept its mouth open to catch its food. Special bones in the back of its mouth called **gill rakers** caught its food. It ate tiny plants and animals called plankton. Whale sharks—the largest fish alive today—catch plankton in exactly the same way. Unlike whale sharks, though, *Leedsichthys* had a skeleton made of bone instead of **cartilage**.

A *Leedsichthys* fossil was found in England. When it was first discovered, scientists mistakenly thought it was parts from a dinosaur.

Length: up to 54 feet

When: Middle Jurassic period—165 to 152 million years ago

Where: Europe and South America

It ate: plankton

It was the size of: two school buses end to end

GUANLONG

SAY IT! Gwan-LONG

Guanlong was a relative of *Tyrannosaurus rex*, but it lived 92 million years earlier. The name *Guanlong* means "crown dragon" after the large crest on its head. This crest would have been brightly colored on the males to attract a mate or threaten a rival.

Guanlong could lose and regrow its teeth over and over again, like sharks do today!

It may have been covered in small, fuzzy feathers that helped it stay warm.

Length: 10 feet

Height: 4 feet

Weight: 200 pounds

When: Late Jurassic period—161 to 155 million years

Where: the forests of China

It ate: other dinosaurs and reptiles

It was the size of: a tiger

Unlike the *T. rex*, *Guanlong* had three fingers instead of two on each hand.

Its long tail helped it balance. It could have been used as a weapon, too!

YANGCHUANOSAURUS

SAY IT! Yang-CHEW-ON-oh-SAWR-us

Yangchuanosaurus gets its name from Yangchuan, China, where it was found. It had long arms with three large claws on each hand. *Yangchuanosaurus* had small horns over its eyes, and may have had very good eyesight. It was also large and fast, making it the most feared carnivore in the area.

Yangchuanosaurus **had serrated teeth that were used to cut meat.**

Females protected their eggs by digging a nest and covering it with plants.

Length: 35 feet

Height: 10 feet

Weight: 5,000 pounds

When: Late Jurassic period 161 to 155 million years ago

Where: the forests of China

It ate: small, medium, and large plant-eating dinosaurs

It was the size of: a school bus

CAIHONG

SAY IT! Ki-hong

JEHOLOPTERUS

SAY IT! ja-hole-OP-tur-us

Wingspan: about 3 feet

When: Late Jurassic period—161 million years ago

Where: China

It ate: maybe small reptiles or other small, feathered dinosaurs

It was the size of: a duck

Wingspan: 2.5 feet

When: Late Jurassic period—160 million years ago

Where: China

It ate: insects or fish

It was the size of: a duck

The hard parts of an animal, like bones and teeth, are what usually become fossils. *Jeholopterus* is a special fossil that has bones as well as soft parts, like skin from the wings. This pterosaur lived around the same time as *Caihong*, a small dinosaur with amazing colors! Pigment cells called **melanosomes** in fossils tell us that *Caihong*'s feathers were **iridescent**!

In Chinese, *Caihong* means "rainbow."

Caihong likely glided from tree to tree, just like flying squirrels do today.

Jeholopterus was covered in pycnofibers (PICK-no-FI-burs), which look like fluffy hair! Pycnofibers kept little *Jeholopterus* warm, just like hair would.

It was gray with black-and-white-speckled wings and had a bright red crest of feathers on its head.

ANCHIORNIS

SAY IT! ang-key-OR-niss

Anchiornis was a feathered dinosaur from China. Its fossils have taught paleontologists many important facts—especially about color. Instead of studying only one feather from the fossil of *Anchiornis*, paleontologists studied different feathers from all over its body. This taught them that *Anchiornis* had many colors on its body, like some modern birds!

Anchiornis spat out **gastric pellets**—just like owls and other predatory birds do today!

Anchiornis means "near bird," because it was an important fossil for learning how small meat-eating dinosaurs evolved to birds.

Wingspan: about 3 feet

When: Late Jurassic period—160 million years ago

Where: China

It ate: lizards and fish

It was the size of: a crow

YI

Yi belonged to one of the weirdest groups of dinosaur: scansoriopterygidae (scan-sore-e-OP-tur-RIDGE-ah-day). With a short head and a small, round snout, *Yi* had only a few angled teeth at the front of its mouth. Like a pterosaur, *Yi* had a very long finger that supported much of the skin of the wing. It also had a rod of cartilage in the middle of the wing to stiffen it and provide support.

In Chinese, *Yi*'s full scientific name— *Yi qi*— means "strange wing."

Wingspan: 20 inches

When: Middle and Late Jurassic period— 160 million years ago

Where: China

It ate: insects

It was the size of: a crow

Dakosaurus means "biter lizard" because of its big teeth.

DAKOSAURUS

SAY IT! DAH-ko-SORE-us

Dakosaurus belonged to a special group of marine crocodiles that lived their entire lives in the sea. They gave birth to their babies in the ocean as well. *Dakosaurus* had four short flippers. It used these flippers and a powerful tail to **ambush** and catch prey. It had big sharp teeth that were shaped like steak knives, perfect for biting and eating meat.

Too much salt is a problem for marine animals. Like marine animals today, the skull of *Dakosaurus* has space to store and remove extra salt from ocean water.

Length: 15 feet

When: Late Jurassic to Early Cretaceous periods—157 to 137 million years ago

Where: Europe and South America

It ate: large fish and other marine reptiles

It was as long as: a soccer goalpost

ALLOSAURUS

SAY IT! AL-oh-SAWR-us

CERATOSAURUS

SAY IT! Suh-RAT-oh-SAWR-us

Length: 39 feet

Height: 16 feet

Weight: 6,000 pounds

When: Late Jurassic period—155 to 150 million years ago

Where: the forests of Colorado, New Mexico, Utah, and Wyoming in the United States, and Portugal

It ate: small, medium, and large plant-eating dinosaurs

It was the size of: a city bus

Length: 23 feet

Height: 7 feet

Weight: 1,000 pounds

When: Late Jurassic period—155 to 150 million years ago

Where: the forests of Colorado and Utah in the United States, and possibly Tanzania in Africa

It ate: small and medium plant-eating dinosaurs and fish

It was the size of: a killer whale

Ceratosaurus and *Allosaurus* were two deadly giant carnivores. *Ceratosaurus* had a blade on its nose, a horn over each eye, and long, thin upper teeth that were perfect for slicing into prey. *Allosaurus* had powerful arms with three-clawed fingers.

BRACHIOSAURUS

SAY IT! BRAK-ee-oh-SAWR-us

DIPLODOCUS

SAY IT! DIPLO-dock-us

BRACHIOSAURUS	DIPLODOCUS
Length: 70 feet	**Length:** 87 feet
Height: 30 feet	**Height:** 14 feet
Weight: 115,000 pounds	**Weight:** 24,000 pounds
When: Late Jurassic period—155 to 150 million years ago	**When:** Late Jurassic period—155 to 150 million years ago
Where: the forests of Colorado and Utah in the United States, and Tanzania	**Where:** the forests of Colorado, Utah, Montana, and Wyoming in the United States
It ate: plants	**It ate:** plants
It was the size of: a three-story building	**It was the size of:** three school buses lined up end to end

During the Late Jurassic Period, North America was home to the giant sauropods *Brachiosaurus* and *Diplodocus*. They lived together in the same ecosystems. *Brachiosaurus* was taller and heavier, while *Diplodocus* was much longer. *Brachiosaurus* used its long neck to eat leaves from the tops of the tallest trees. *Diplodocus* ate plants that grew lower to the ground, but it could also rear up to reach higher. Eating at different levels allowed these two giants to live in the same forests.

STEGOSAURUS

SAY IT! STEG-oh-SAWR-us

Stegosaurus was the largest member of the stegosaur family. It had two rows of plates on its back and four spikes on its tail. No one knows exactly what the plates were for. Paleontologists believe that they helped warm up the *Stegosaurus* by capturing the rays of the sun.

The plates could also have had large spots that looked like eyes to scare away predators. Along with its powerful tail spikes, *Stegosaurus* had small pieces of bone called **osteoderms** covering its neck. This helped protect it from attackers.

Length: 30 feet

Height: 14 feet

Weight: 11,000 pounds

When: Late Jurassic period—155 to 150 million years ago

Where: the forests of western North America and Portugal

It ate: plants

It was the size of: a small school bus

Its brain was about the size of two Ping-Pong balls.

COMPSOGNATHUS

SAY IT! COMP-soh-NAY-thus

When the *Compsognathus* was first discovered, many people thought it was the smallest dinosaur. They realized later that those first bones were from a baby. As adults, *Compsognathus* were dangerous carnivores. They may have hunted in packs and eaten animals that washed ashore on the beaches they lived near.

Paleontologists once thought this dinosaur had two fingers on each hand, but it actually had three.

Length: 4 feet

Height: 2 feet

Weight: 20 pounds

When: Late Jurassic period—155 to 145 million years ago

Where: the shores and forests of Europe

It ate: insects, fish, small reptiles, eggs, and baby dinosaurs

It was the size of: a turkey

ARCHAEOPTERYX

SAY IT! ahr-key-OP-tur-icks

Archaeopteryx is perhaps the most famous fossil of all time. This **transitional fossil** proved that birds evolved from dinosaurs. When it was first discovered, scientists were debating the origin of birds. *Archaeopteryx* surprised everyone because it had features of both dinosaurs and birds. It was a small, meat-eating dinosaur with teeth, long arms, claws, a long tail, and feathered wings! Some paleontologists think that *Archaeopteryx* used its claws to climb up trees, then jumped and glided from tree to tree.

You can see the most famous *Archaeopteryx* fossil, known as the "Berlin Specimen," at the Berlin Museum of Natural History in Germany.

Wingspan: 2 feet

When: Late Jurassic period—150 to 148 million years ago

Where: Germany

It ate: small reptiles, and maybe even other small dinosaurs

It was the size of: a crow

Pterodactylus lived alongside *Archaeopteryx.*

PTERODACTYLUS

SAY IT! tare-o-DACK-tull-us

The famous *Pterodactylus* was the first pterosaur ever found. When it was discovered, scientists were not sure what kind of animal it was. Some thought *Pterodactylus* was a sea creature. Others thought it might have been a flying **marsupial**, the group of animals that kangaroos and koalas belong to. When scientists first made drawings to imagine what *Pterodactylus* looked like when it was alive, they modeled their designs after a bat!

French scientist Georges Cuvier originally called it "Ptéro-Dactyle." Because scientific names need to be in Latin, the name was changed from *Pterodactyl* to *Pterodactylus*.

Wingspan: about 3 feet

When: Late Jurassic period—150 to 148 million years ago

Where: Germany

It ate: fish and other small animals

It was the size of: a raven

PART THREE

CRETACEOUS PERIOD

The end of the Mesozoic Era is called the Cretaceous Period. The Cretaceous Period lasted from 145 million to 66 million years ago. This is when some famous dinosaurs, like *Velociraptor*, *Triceratops*, and *Tyrannosaurus rex* all lived.

PSITTACOSAURUS

SAY IT! sih-TACK-oh-SAWR-us

Psittacosaurus was a small cousin of *Triceratops* that walked on two legs instead of four. Using lasers, paleontologists have been able to identify the actual color of its skin! *Psittacosaurus* had a dark-colored back and light-colored stomach, which made it hard for predators to see it. This dinosaur was a very good parent and would protect its young against danger. Even the babies were fast enough to outrun many carnivores. It had long, whisker-like feathers on its tail that could be used to signal to other members of the family or chase away flies and mosquitoes.

Length: 6 feet

Height: 2 feet

Weight: 40 pounds

When: Early Cretaceous period—140 to 99 million years ago

Where: the forests and meadows of Mongolia and China

It ate: plants

It was the size of: a small dog

BARYONYX

SAY IT! BARE-ee-ON-icks

Baryonyx had huge claws, long and sharp teeth, and a head shaped like a crocodile's. It is closely related to *Spinosaurus. Baryonyx* may have spent most of its time in the water, where it used its very large thumb claw to grab fish. Paleontologists know that it ate fish because fish scales were found in its stomach area. So were the bones of a plant-eating dinosaur!

Length: 32 feet

Height: 8 feet

Weight: 2,700 pounds

When: Early Cretaceous period—140 to 112 million years ago

Where: near the lakes and rivers of Spain and England

It ate: fish, turtles, and small and medium plant-eating dinosaurs

It was the size of: a school bus

Baryonyx had 95 teeth, which was way more than most other meat eaters.

IGUANODON

SAY IT! ig-WAN-oh-DON

Iguanodon was among the first dinosaurs ever found, and the second to receive a name. The name means "iguana tooth" because its teeth were shaped like those of modern iguanas. The most amazing feature of *Iguanodon* was the large thumb spike on each hand. When it was first discovered, paleontologists thought the spike was a horn from the nose. Later discoveries showed that it was actually attached to the hand. With its large, powerful body and excellent weapons, *Iguanodon* was able to live in many places throughout the world.

It could walk on two legs or four.

Length: 43 feet

Height: 10 feet

Weight: 7,500 pounds

When: Early Cretaceous period—140 to 112 million years ago

Where: the forests and swamps of Europe, China, and North America

It ate: plants

It was the size of: a large bus

WUERHOSAURUS

SAY IT! woo-AIR-ho-SAWR-us

Wuerhosaurus may have been the last remaining member of the stegosaur family. All its relatives died out at the end of the Jurassic Period, but it survived into the Early Cretaceous Period. Like its relatives, it had plates on its back and spikes on its tail. But its plates seem to have been much shorter than the plates on other stegosaurs. It had a small brain, but it was smart enough to survive longer than all other stegosaurs.

It may have had long spikes on its shoulders for defense.

Wuerhosaurus had five toes on its front feet, but only three on the back.

Length: 20 feet

Height: 10 feet

Weight: 8,000 pounds

When: Early Cretaceous period—135 to 120 million years ago

Where: the forest and swamps of China

It ate: plants

It was the size of: a van

Its rear legs were much longer than its front legs.

It may have been able to run over 30 miles per hour!

It had three fingers on each hand.

CONCAVENATOR

SAY IT! Con-CAVE-uh-nay-tor

Concavenator is one of the strangest meat eaters ever discovered. This medium-size dinosaur had a large, pointy hump on its hips and bumps on its arms called quill knobs. The hump could have been used to help cool the *Concavenator* when it was hot, or to attract a mate. The quill knobs may have held long feathers that hung down from the arms. Paleontologists do not know for sure what these features were used for, but they do know that *Concavenator* was a very dangerous carnivore.

Concavenator laid eggs, like a bird.

Length: 20 feet

Height: 5 feet

Weight: 5,000 pounds

When: Early Cretaceous period—130 to 120 million years ago

Where: the lowlands and forests of Spain and Europe

It ate: small and medium plant-eating dinosaurs

It was the size of: an SUV

AMARGASAURUS

SAY IT! a-MARG-a-SAWR-us

Amargasaurus had two rows of long spikes that ran down its neck to its shoulders. The spikes may have been used as weapons against predators. The tallest spike was over two feet long! By lowering its head, *Amargasaurus* could point the spikes at an attacker to keep it away. The spikes may have been brightly colored as warnings to other dinosaurs. While these spikes were perfect for defense, they prevented *Amargasaurus* from bending its neck upward to reach higher into trees. Because the spikes would have stabbed into its own back, it could only eat leaves and plants that grew lower to the ground.

Amargasaurus had short legs and was very slow.

Length: 40 feet

Height: 10 feet

Weight: 6,000 pounds

When: Early Cretaceous period— 130 to 120 million years ago

Where: the forests and swamps of Argentina

It ate: plants

It was the size of: a city bus

GASTONIA

SAY IT! gas-TONE-ee-uh

Gastonia was a medium-size member of the ankylosaur family. It had spikes, horns, and osteoderms covering its back, sides, and tail. But it did not have a heavy tail club like other ankylosaurs. It was a slow-moving herbivore that was built like a tank. Its heavy body armor and spikes protected it from the deadly *Utahraptor* that lived in its environment. *Gastonia*'s belly was unprotected, so it had to keep low to the ground when under attack. Luckily, it was so heavy that carnivores like *Utahraptor* weren't strong enough to flip it over.

Length: 20 feet

Height: 3 feet

Weight: 3,000 pounds

When: Early Cretaceous period— 130 to 125 million years ago

Where: the forests of Utah in the United States

It ate: plants

It was the size of: a small car

Gastonia had a flat beak that it used to cut through tough plants.

ACROCANTHOSAURUS

SAY IT! ACK-row-CAN-tho-SAR-us

Acrocanthosaurus, or "high-spined lizard," gets its name from the large, raised ridge on its neck and back. The ridge may have been used to make it look larger to rivals. It may also have been used to cool down or warm up its body. *Acrocanthosaurus* is known as a head hunter because it caught its prey with its mouth, then used its claws to hold on to it. Fossils show that it hunted the sauropods.

Acrocanthosaurus reached its adult size by 12 years old.

Length: 39 feet

Height: 11 feet

Weight: 15,000 pounds

When: Early to Late Cretaceous period—112 to 93 million years ago

Where: the forests of Algeria, Egypt, Morocco, and Niger

It ate: plant-eating dinosaurs of all sizes

It was the size of: a city bus

Microraptor probably had shiny black feathers.

Confuciusornis had claws on its hands, unlike most birds today.

Confuciusornis was named in honor of the Chinese philosopher Confucius.

CONFUCIUSORNIS

SAY IT! kun-FEW-sush-OR-niss

MICRORAPTOR

SAY IT! MY-crow-RAP-tor

Wingspan: 3 feet

When: Early Cretaceous period—120 million years ago

Where: China

It ate: small mammals, birds, lizards, and fish

It was the size of: a raven

Wingspan: about 2 feet

When: Early Cretaceous period—125 to 120 million years ago

Where: China

It ate: fish

It was the size of: a pigeon

Confuciusornis is the oldest-known bird to have a beak like modern birds. The male had two tail feathers that were nearly as long as its entire body!

The dinosaur *Microraptor* lived alongside *Confuciusornis*. Like other birds, *Microraptor* had one set of wings on its arms, but it also had another pair on its legs. Paleontologists think that *Microraptor* used its four wings to glide from tree to tree.

NEMICOLOPTERUS

SAY IT! nim-e-coal-OP-tur-us

We often think that all prehistoric creatures were gigantic, but that's not true! Many were tiny, and *Nemicolopterus* was likely the smallest pterosaur. The body of *Nemicolopterus* was only about 2 inches long. Many other forest-dwelling pterosaurs had teeth for catching insects and small reptiles, but *Nemicolopterus* didn't. So, what did it eat? Perhaps small insects that it didn't need teeth to catch. Or maybe it ate fruit or leaves.

Nemicolopterus lived in lush inland forests filled with many different kinds of pterosaurs and dinosaurs.

Wingspan: 10 inches

When: Early Cretaceous period—120 million years ago

Where: the forests of ancient China

It ate: insects and fruit

It was the size of: a robin

Paleontologists don't know if *Nemicolopterus* is the smallest pterosaur or just a baby of another pterosaur.

SAUROPELTA

SAY IT! SAWR-oh-PELT-ah

Sauropelta is known for the huge spikes on its shoulders. These spikes, along with its thick skin and pieces of body armor, made it safe from any attack. *Sauropelta* was a medium-size herbivore and one of the earliest-known members of the ankylosaur family. Because of its body armor, it weighed as much as an elephant and moved very slowly. But it may have been a good swimmer that was able to float in water.

Length: 25 feet

Height: 4 feet

Weight: 3,300 pounds

When: Early Cretaceous period—118 to 110 million years ago

Where: the forests and swamps of Wyoming, Montana, and Utah in the United States

It ate: plants

It was the size of: a pickup truck

Its tail was half as long as the rest of its body.

UTAHRAPTOR

SAY IT! YOU-taw-RAP-tur

Raptors were among the smartest and most dangerous meat-eating dinosaurs that ever lived. The family name for raptors is **dromaeosaurs** (droe-MAY-us-sawrs). *Utahraptor* was the biggest and strongest of all raptors. It had powerful arms with long claws that could grab and shred its prey. Its curved foot claw could slice through the thick skin of any dinosaur. Because it was so large and heavy, *Utahraptor* was not very fast.

Its curved foot claw was almost 15 inches long!

Length: 23 feet

Height: 8 feet

Weight: 2,000 pounds

When: Early Cretaceous period—118 to 110 million years ago

Where: the forests and beaches of Utah in the United States

It ate: medium and large plant-eating dinosaurs

It was the size of: an SUV

Utahraptor is one of the oldest members of the raptor family.

It's the official state dinosaur of Utah.

Forward-facing eyes helped *Deinonychus* see and catch running prey.

DEINONYCHUS

SAY IT! Dye-NON-ih-kus

Deinonychus was a fast, dangerous dinosaur that used the deadly curved claws on its feet to slice open its prey. It could hunt alone or in groups.

Its jaws were not very strong, so it used its hands to tear off pieces of meat.

Its tail was so stiff that it couldn't even wiggle it!

Length: 13 feet

Height: 3 feet

Weight: 150 pounds

When: Early Cretaceous period—118 to 110 million years ago

Where: the forests of Utah in the United States

It ate: plant-eating dinosaurs of all sizes

It was the size of: a tiger

ORNITHOCHEIRUS

SAY IT! or-nith-O-ki-russ

The name *Ornithocheirus* means "bird hand." When *Ornithocheirus* fossils were first found, paleontologists thought that these pterosaurs were the direct ancestors of birds. We now know that pterosaurs and birds are not related! Even though both creatures have the bones of the hand and finger in their wings, a pterosaur's wing is very different from a bird's wing.

Wingspan: 16 feet

When: Early Cretaceous period—113 to 110 million years ago

Where: United Kingdom

It ate: fish

Its wingspan was the size of: a giraffe

Ornithocheirus may have soared across the ancient seas, just like albatrosses do today.

Instead of a fancy head crest, *Ornithocheirus* had a long bill with a rounded tip.

It may have dipped its beak in the water to snag fish or it may have dived into the water to catch them.

XIPHACTINUS

SAY IT! za-FACT-ta-niss

Xiphactinus was a large fish. This predator lived in the ancient seas during the time of the dinosaurs. It may have lived and traveled in schools, just like many fish do today. *Xiphactinus* had a big appetite. One famous fossil found in the 1950s was a 13-foot *Xiphactinus* with a 6-foot-long fish stuck inside it! This *Xiphactinus* likely choked from trying to eat a fish that was too big.

Xiphactinus fossils were found in Kansas, USA. During the Cretaceous Period, there was an ocean in the middle of North America.

Xiphactinus may have weighed nearly 1,000 pounds. That's heavier than a grand piano.

Length: up to 20 feet

When: Early to Late Cretaceous period—112 to 66 million years ago

Where: North and South America, Europe, and Australia

It ate: other fish

It was the size of: a giraffe

CARCHARODONTOSAURUS

SAY IT! Car-CAR-oh-don-toe-SAWR-us

The name *Carcharodontosaurus* means "shark-toothed lizard." This carnivore had sharklike teeth that could slice through the thickest skin of any dinosaur. It also had a powerful bite, strong neck, and sharp claws. These features allowed it to hunt the biggest of all dinosaurs: sauropods. *Carcharodontosaurus* also had a heavy body that was made for battle. When it attacked, it rushed in with its mouth open and grabbed its prey. It was one of the top hunters of Africa. Even giant meat eaters like *Spinosaurus* probably stayed away.

Length: 39 feet

Height: 11 feet

Weight: 15,000 pounds

When: Early to Late Cretaceous period—112 to 93 million years ago

Where: the forests of Algeria, Egypt, Morocco, and Niger

It ate: plant-eating dinosaurs of all sizes

It was the size of: a city bus

LUDODACTYLUS

SAY IT! lu-doh-DACK-tull-us

Ludodactylus looked a lot like another pterosaur called *Pteranodon*—except it had teeth. In fact, *Ludodactylus* was the first pterosaur found that had both a big head crest and teeth. We have only one fossil of *Ludodactylus*, which has a leaf stuck in its mouth! Paleontologists believe that this *Ludodactylus* saw the leaf floating on the water and mistook it for a fish. The leaf then got stuck in its mouth, making it hard for *Ludodactylus* to catch fish.

The leaf stuck in its mouth was from a yucca plant. Yucca plants are still around today!

The second part of *Ludodactylus*'s scientific name is *sibbicki*, in honor of famous paleoartist John Sibbick.

Wingspan: 13 feet

When: Early Cretaceous period—112 million years ago

Where: Brazil

It ate: fish

It was the size of: a dolphin

TUPANDACTYLUS

SAY IT! two-pan-DAK-tul-us

Imagine if your ring fingers were longer than your body—that's what the wing of *Tupandactylus* was like! Like all pterosaurs, its wing is made of one long finger bone. *Tupandactylus* had short, deep jaws and a long skull with a crest of **keratin** on top. It lived along the edge of a giant, ancient lake. Some paleontologists believe that *Tupandactylus* used its crest like a sail to glide and steer above the waves.

Paleontologists don't know what *Tupandactylus*'s crest was for. Was it to control their direction when flying or maybe help identify other species? Or was it just for display, similar to a peacock's tail?

Wingspan: 16 feet

When: Early Cretaceous period—112 million years ago

Where: Brazil

It ate: fruit and tough seeds, or fish

It was the size of: a car

Tupandactylus had two bones sticking out from its skull. Between them was keratin—the same stuff our fingernails are made of!

Some paleontologists think that *Thalassodromeus* is not its own species but rather a fully grown pterosaur called *Tupuxuara*.

THALASSODROMEUS

SAY IT! tha-lass-o-DRO-me-us

The name *Thalassodromeus* means "sea runner." Paleontologists who named this pterosaur thought that it flew fast above the water and skimmed fish. But the shape of *Thalassodromeus*'s bill is very different from the bills of water-skimming birds today. New research suggests that *Thalassodromeus* flew over land and used its bill to catch smaller land animals and even some small dinosaurs.

Wingspan: 17 feet

When: Early Cretaceous period—110 million years ago

Where: Brazil

It ate: small animals

Its wingspan was the size of: a hippopotamus

The second part of *Thalassodromeus*'s scientific name is *sethi*, in honor of the Egyptian god Seth.

The giant triangular head crest of *Thalassodromeus* makes it one of the biggest pterosaur skulls.

PTERODAUSTRO

SAY IT! tear-o-DAW-stro

Pterodaustro was a pterosaur with an unusual bill. Its long jaws were curved and filled with bristlelike teeth. There's a flying animal today that also has curved, bristle-filled jaws—the flamingo! Because their jaws are so similar, paleontologists think that *Pterodaustro* sifted through the water for food just like a flamingo does. From studying the eyes of *Pterodaustro,* paleontologists found that this creature was most active in the evenings, just like many geese, ducks, and swans are today.

Flamingos are pink because of the colors in the tiny shrimp and algae they eat. This means *Pterodaustro* might have been pink as well.

Wingspan: 4.5 feet

When: Early Cretaceous period—105 million years ago

Where: Argentina

It ate: small animals

Its wingspan was the size of: a 10-year-old child

Pterodaustro was one of the first pterosaurs discovered in South America.

Paleontologists found a fossil of a *Pterodaustro* egg with an embryo inside it.

SAUROPOSEIDON

SAY IT! SOR-oh-po-SIE-don

Sauroposeidon was a gigantic herbivore that used its long neck to reach into the tallest trees for food. Many footprints belonging to *Sauroposeidon* have been found in Texas, USA. It preferred to live along the coast of the shallow seas that once covered most of North America. Early paleontologists thought that the long necks of sauropods allowed them to live in water, but dinosaurs like *Sauroposeidon* could not have lived liked this. The pressure of the water would have made it impossible for it to breathe. It also had teeth that were made for chewing tough land plants, not soft plants that lived in the water.

Length: 99 feet

Height: 40 feet

Weight: 100,000 pounds

When: Early Cretaceous period—100 to 140 million years ago

It ate: plants

Where: the coasts and forests of Texas, Oklahoma, and Wyoming in the United States

It was the size of: a nine-story building

RUGOPS

SAY IT! ROO-gops

Rugops means "wrinkle face"! The name comes from its skull that was covered in bumps. A male *Rugops* probably had colorful markings on its head. Although it may have looked dangerous, this medium-size carnivore had thin skull bones, a weak bite, and short arms. It probably didn't hunt its own prey. Instead, it would steal food from smaller predators, or act like a **scavenger** by eating animals that were already dead.

Length: 17 feet

Height: 4 feet

Weight: 900 pounds

When: Late Cretaceous period—99 to 90 million years ago

Where: the coast of Niger

It ate: small and medium plant-eating dinosaurs

It was the size of: an SUV

It may have been able to change the color of its face when it was angry or scared.

ARGENTINOSAURUS

SAY IT! AR-jen-TEE-no-SAWR-us

Argentinosaurus may have been the largest animal that ever walked the Earth. It weighed more than 60 elephants. Its huge body was like a giant bulldozer that could push through the forests. *Argentinosaurus* may have been able to only walk five miles per hour, but it was so strong it could snap any tree in front of it. It may have eaten up to 1,000 pounds of food every day! It probably even ate in the dark, sleeping only a few hours each night. No one knows why *Argentinosaurus* grew so large. It may have been for protection against carnivores, or because there was so much food available. No other land animal has ever reached its giant size.

Length: 120 feet

Height: 48 feet

Weight: 200,000 pounds

When: Late Cretaceous period—97 to 93 million years ago

Where: the forests of Argentina

It ate: plants

It was the size of: five city buses lined up end to end

PACHYRHINOSAURUS

SAY IT! **PACK-ee-RINE-oh-SAWR-us**

TRICERATOPS

SAY IT! **try-SER-uh-tops**

Length: 26 feet	**Length:** 30 feet
Height: 10 feet	**Height:** 12 feet
Weight: 8,000 pounds	**Weight:** 25,000 pounds
When: Late Cretaceous period—88 to 66 million years ago	**When:** Late Cretaceous period—66 to 65 million years ago
Where: the forests and swamps of Canada and Alaska, USA	**Where:** the forests and swamps of the Western United States and Canada
It ate: plants	**It ate:** plants
It was the size of: a pickup truck	**It was the size of:** a pickup truck

During the Late Cretaceous Period, North America was home to several members of the ceratopsian family, including *Triceratops* and *Pachyrhinosaurus*. Although these herbivores looked different, they were related and may have traveled together. When danger approached, they could take on the largest predators of their time—even *Tyrannosaurus rex*!

In movies, *Pteranodon* is shown picking up things with its feet like an eagle, but its feet were too small and weak to do this.

PTERANODON

SAY IT! ta-RAN-oh-don

We know more about *Pteranodon* than any other pterosaur because we have hundreds of fossils of this large flying creature. It had a long, thin bill and sickle-shaped crest. *Pteranodon* lived at the edge of an ancient ocean in the middle of North America. A female was about half the size of a male. Only the males had a giant crest on the back of their heads. This is just like how male deer have antlers but females don't. The crest of the male *Pteranodon* may have been used to attract a mate.

Pteranodon fossils have been found with digested fish inside.

Wingspan: 22 feet

When: Late Cretaceous period—86 to 84 million years ago

Where: North America

It ate: fish

Its wingspan was the size of: a two-story building

NYCTOSAURUS

SAY IT! nick-toe-SORE-us

Nyctosaurus has one of the coolest head crests of all pterosaurs. Its forked crest was twice as long as its body! Its crest changed and grew longer as it became an adult. Paleontologists used to think that there was skin between the bone crest—just like the sail on a sailboat. However, when paleontologists studied how crests function in flight, they determined that a skin-sail would not help *Nyctosaurus*.

It was discovered by the famous paleontologist Othniel Charles Marsh, who also discovered *Pteranodon*.

Wingspan: 6 feet

When: Late Cretaceous period—85 to 84 million years ago

Where: United States

It ate: fish

Its wingspan was the size of: an adult

SAICHANIA

SAY IT! Sie-CAN-ee-uh

This medium-size ankylosaur was heavily armored. It had layers of thick, bony plates that covered its neck, sides, back, and legs. This protected it from all but the largest carnivores. *Saichania* could live in several different ecosystems, including the dry, hot desert. Its nose would cool the hot desert air when it breathed in so it wouldn't overheat. Like a camel, it could go for a long time without drinking water.

Length: 23 feet

Height: 4 feet

Weight: 4,000 pounds

When: Late Cretaceous period—85 to 70 million years ago

Where: the desert areas of Mongolia

It ate: plants

It was the size of: a pickup truck

Its jaws could chew tough desert plants as well as soft ferns.

VELOCIRAPTOR

SAY IT! Vuh-LAH-su-RAP-tor

Velociraptor was one of the fastest members of the dromaeosaur family. These small but deadly dinosaurs may have hunted in packs to bring down larger prey. Even though it had feathers on its arms, *Velociraptor* was too heavy to fly. The feathers may have been used to keep warm at night.

Like its bird cousins, *Velociraptor* had a wishbone!

Its large, curved foot claw is called the "killing claw."

Length: 6 feet

Height: 2 feet

Weight: 35 pounds

When: Late Cretaceous period—85 to 70 million years ago

Where: the deserts of Mongolia

It ate: small and medium plant-eating dinosaurs

It was the size of: a turkey

Hesperornis was found by the famous paleontologist Othniel Charles Marsh.

HESPERORNIS

SAY IT! Hess-purr-OR-niss

Imagine a cross between a penguin and a duck. Now give that bird some teeth. That's probably what *Hesperornis* looked like. Similar to penguins, *Hesperornis* was flightless and swam in the ocean to catch fish. But instead of flapping its wings to swim, *Hesperornis* moved through the water with large, paddlelike feet, like a duck or loon. Unlike penguins, which live in cold climates, *Hesperornis* lived in warm tropical areas similar to the Southeastern United States.

Wingspan: unknown

When: Early Cretaceous period—83 to 78 million years ago

Where: North America

It ate: fish

It was the size of: an adult human

It was the first fossil bird found with teeth!

Today, paleontologists can find *Hesperornis* fossils along the coast of an ancient ocean that split North America in two.

LABOCANIA

SAY IT! Lah-boh-CAN-ee-uh

Labocania was a cousin of *Tyrannosaurus rex*, but it was not as large or powerful. It was fast, though, and able to chase down and catch its prey. Using its sharp teeth and long claws, *Labocania* could attack all but the biggest plant-eating dinosaurs.

Labocania used its thick skull bones to knock down prey.

It had two fingers on each hand, like *T. rex*.

Length: 25 feet

Height: 6 feet

Weight: 3,000 pounds

When: Late Cretaceous period—83 to 70 million years ago

Where: the forests of Mexico

It ate: small and medium plant-eating dinosaurs

It was the size of: an elephant

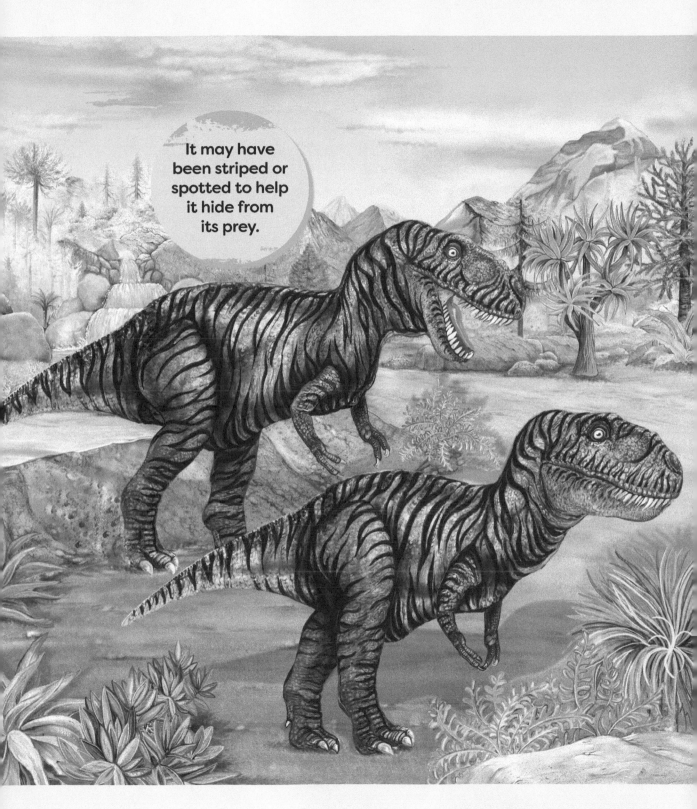

Archelon means "first turtle," because it was the first sea turtle fossil ever discovered.

ARCHELON

SAY IT! ARK-ah-lawn

Archelon was the largest sea turtle that ever lived. Its shell was as big as a dinner table! While *Archelon*'s body and shell looked a lot like the giant sea turtles alive today, its head was different. *Archelon* had a curved beak that looked almost like a parrot's beak. It swam in the Western Interior Seaway—a warm, shallow ocean that used to be in the middle of North America.

Archelon probably went extinct when the Western Interior Seaway began to dry up.

Length: 15 feet

When: Late Cretaceous period—80 to 74 million years ago

Where: North America

It ate: squid and jellyfish

It was the size of: a car

BAMBIRAPTOR

SAY IT! BAM-be-RAP-tur

Bambiraptor was one of the smaller members of the raptor family. Paleontologists believe that it was covered in feathers like its modern cousins: hawks, eagles, and owls. This dinosaur could jump down on unsuspecting prey!

Bambiraptor slashed prey with a curved claw on its foot.

It used its stiff tail for balance.

Length: 3 feet

Height: 2 feet

Weight: 4 pounds

When: Late Cretaceous period—80 to 72 million years ago

Where: the forests and meadows of Montana in the United States

It ate: insects, eggs, small reptiles, and baby dinosaurs

It was the size of: a cat

The first *Bambiraptor* was found by a 14-year-old boy who was hunting fossils in Montana, USA!

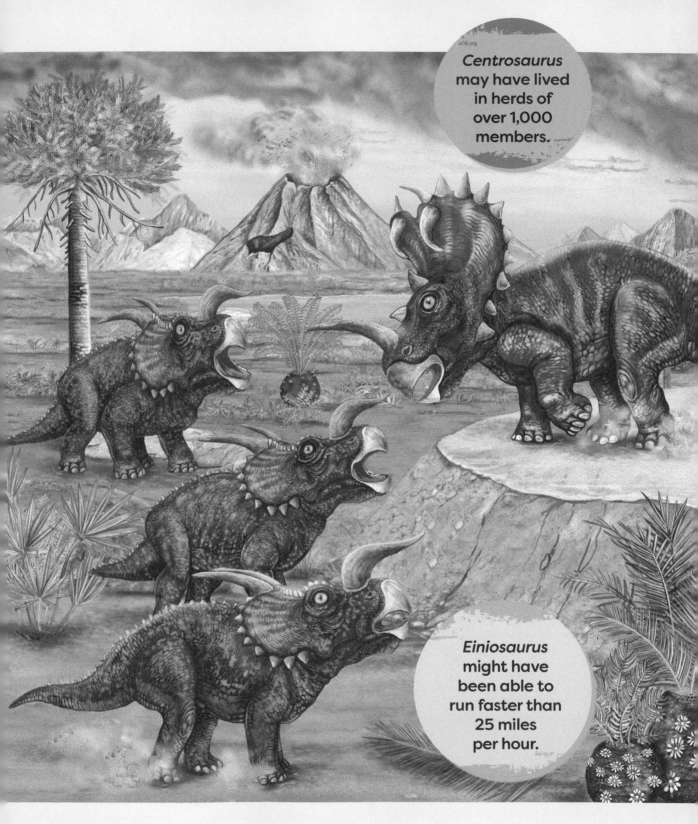

Centrosaurus may have lived in herds of over 1,000 members.

Einiosaurus might have been able to run faster than 25 miles per hour.

CENTROSAURUS

SAY IT! SEN-trow-SAWR-us

EINIOSAURUS

SAY IT! i-NEE-oh-SAWR-us

Length: 19 feet

Height: 6 feet

Weight: 6,000 pounds

When: Late Cretaceous period—80 to 72 million years ago

Where: the forests of Canada

It ate: plants

It was the size of: a pickup truck

Length: 20 feet

Height: 5 feet

Weight: 3,000 pounds

When: Late Cretaceous period—80 to 72 million years ago

Where: the forests of Montana and possibly Canada

It ate: plants

It was the size of: a pickup truck

Centrosaurus and *Einiosaurus* were members of the ceratopsian family. These two did not have large horns over their eyes like most ceratopsians. Instead, they each had a long nose horn. Many ceratopsians lived in herds and may have even lived with other types of horned dinosaurs. By living in groups, they were better protected against large carnivores.

EDMONTOSAURUS

SAY IT! ed-MON-toe-SAWR-us

LAMBEOSAURUS

SAY IT! lam-BEE-oh-SAWR-us

Length: 40 feet

Height: 13 feet

Weight: 8,500 pounds

When: Late Cretaceous period—72 to 65 million years ago

Where: the forests and swamps of the Western United States and Canada

It ate: plants

It was the size of: a bus

Length: 49 feet

Height: 13 feet

Weight: 9,100 pounds

When: Late Cretaceous period—80 to 72 million years ago

Where: the swamps and forests of Canada and possibly Mexico

It ate: plants

It was the size of: a tractor

Ornithopods were common dinosaurs during the Cretaceous Period. These birdlike dinosaurs would **migrate** across the country to survive. *Edmontosaurus* and *Lambeosaurus* had very different-looking heads, but they were still closely related. The long, flat beak of *Edmontosaurus* helped it gather large amounts of food. The strange crest of *Lambeosaurus* may have been used to communicate with other members of its family.

PARASAUROLOPHUS

SAY IT! PAIR-uh-SAWR-ohl-OW-fuss

Parasaurolophus is a duck-billed ornithopod. The crest on the back of its skull was over five feet long! Some paleontologists believe that the crest was used to make sound, while others believe it gave *Parasaurolophus* a very powerful sense of smell. *Parasaurolophus* had a flat beak that was perfect for biting large mouthfuls of plants. Although it looked like the beak of a duck, *Parasaurolophus* did not spend a lot of time in the water. It may not even have been a very good swimmer, instead spending its time in the forests.

Length: 33 feet

Height: 12 feet

Weight: 5,000 pounds

When: Late Cretaceous period—80 to 72 million years ago

Where: the forests and swamps of New Mexico and Utah in the United States, and Canada

It ate: plants

It was the size of: a school bus

It could use its tail as a weapon to knock down attackers.

STYRACOSAURUS

SAY IT! sty-RACK-oh-SAWR-us

Styracosaurus means "spiked lizard." It had large spikes on its nose and frill that may have been used as defense weapons. Some spikes were more than two feet long and covered in keratin, which made them very sharp. *Styracosaurus* was a powerful dinosaur that could push down tall trees to reach the leaves. Because of *Styracosaurus*'s strong body and long spikes, meat eaters would stay away from the adults and only attack the babies.

The beak was a powerful weapon and could be used to bite through tough plants.

Length: 18 feet

Height: 6 feet

Weight: 6,000 pounds

When: Late Cretaceous period—80 to 72 million years ago

Where: the forests and swamps of Canada and Montana

It ate: plants

It was the size of: an SUV

SALTASAURUS

SAY IT! SAL-tuh-SAWR-us

Saltasaurus was a medium-size sauropod with a short neck and a long, whiplike tail. It was one of the few sauropods that had osteoderms covering its back. This protected it from both large and small predators. Fossilized *Saltasaurus* eggs have shown that babies were born with osteoderms on their backs as well. Some paleontologists believe that *Saltasaurus* was a good swimmer that may have walked across shallow lakes and rivers, or floated like a boat in deeper water.

It weighed as much as two elephants.

Saltasaurus could eat 500 pounds of plants every day.

Length: 40 feet

Height: 13 feet

Weight: 12,000 pounds

When: Late Cretaceous period—72 to 66 million years ago

Where: the forests of Argentina

It ate: plants

It was the size of: a school bus

DEINOCHEIRUS

SAY IT! Dye-no-KYE-rus

This dinosaur was strange! Its arms were almost eight feet long and there was a large hump on its back. No one knows for sure what the hump was used for. Some paleontologists think it was used to store fat like the hump of a camel. *Deinocheirus* had a long neck and tail. It also had a beak but no teeth. To grind its food, *Deinocheirus* swallowed small stones called **gastroliths**.

Length: 36 feet

Height: 16 feet

Weight: 14,000 pounds

When: Late Cretaceous period— 70 to 68 million years ago

Where: along the rivers and lakes of Mongolia

It ate: fish, small and medium dinosaurs, and possibly plants

It was the size of: a school bus

Deinocheirus **may have been an omnivore, eating both plants and meat.**

GALLIMIMUS

SAY IT! GAL-ee-MY-muss

Gallimimus was one of the fastest and smartest dinosaurs. It could run up to 50 miles per hour to escape larger predators and chase down its prey. *Gallimimus* ate mostly small reptiles, mammals, or eggs, but it may have eaten plants and fruit, too. Because *Gallimimus* had no teeth, it had to swallow whatever it ate whole. Its arms were thin, so it probably used its long neck to reach down and grab its prey.

It lived in herds for protection against larger meat eaters.

Length: 20 feet

Height: 7 feet

Weight: 950 pounds

When: Late Cretaceous period—70 to 68 million years ago

Where: the deserts of Mongolia

It ate: small reptiles, mammals, baby dinosaurs, eggs, and plants

It was the size of: a truck

SHANTUNGOSAURUS

SAY IT! shan-TUNG-oh-SAWR-us

This huge herbivore was slow, but very powerful. The largest member of the ornithopod family, its size and powerful tail prevented most meat eaters from attacking it. Paleontologists do not understand why *Shantungosaurus* grew so large, but it may have been because so much food was available. It might have had up to 1,500 small teeth, which allowed it to eat almost any plant in its environment, even the toughest ones. It would migrate from place to place in search of more food.

Length: 50 feet

Height: 16 feet

Weight: 36,000 pounds

When: Late Cretaceous period—70 to 68 million years ago

Where: the forests and swamps of China

It ate: plants

It was the size of: a fighter jet

It was a good swimmer.

TARBOSAURUS

SAY IT! TAR-bow-SAWR-us

Tarbosaurus was the smaller cousin of *Tyrannosaurus rex*. With powerful jaws and teeth, its bite was strong enough to crush bones! *Tarbosaurus* was heavy and probably couldn't run very fast. This means it may have ambushed its prey instead of chasing it down. It could also steal prey from smaller meat eaters. Some paleontologists even believe *Tarbosaurus* was a scavenger that didn't hunt its prey at all.

Tarbosaurus had an excellent sense of smell.

Length: 33 feet

Height: 14 feet

Weight: 10,000 pounds

When: Late Cretaceous period—70 to 68 million years ago

Where: the forests of Mongolia and China

It ate: large plant-eating dinosaurs

It was the size of: a school bus

QUETZALCOATLUS

SAY IT! KET-zul-koh-AH-tul-us

The giant *Quetzalcoatlus* might be the largest flying animal that ever lived on Earth! It soared above the ancient plains of western North America. *Quetzalcoatlus* is named after the legendary god Quetzalcoatl (KET-zul-koh-AH-tul). Paleontologists aren't sure what this pterosaur ate. Some think it was like a vulture and fed on dead dinosaurs. Some think it grabbed fish when flying low to the water. Others think it walked around and snatched up small animals like baby dinosaurs.

The US military used a model of *Quetzalcoatlus* to design an experimental airplane.

Wingspan: 40 feet

When: Late Cretaceous period—68 to 66 million years ago

Where: Western United States

It ate: dead dinosaurs, fish, or small animals

It was the size of: a small airplane

Once in the air, *Quetzalcoatlus* may have kept its wings stretched out and glided like a giant kite.

Not only was the **wingspan** of *Quetzalcoatlus* huge, but the creature was also very tall when walking on land. A standing *Quetzalcoatlus* was as tall as a giraffe!

ANKYLOSAURUS

SAY IT! an-KIE-low-SAWR-us

Ankylosaurus was the largest of the armored dinosaurs. Its skin was so thick and protected that no meat eater could bite through it. *Ankylosaurus* had a powerful tail club that it used as a weapon. The flexible tail could swing from side to side, and the end was a club made of solid bone. *Ankylosaurus* was so heavy that it could crush anything it hit. It was among the last of the dinosaurs to ever exist. It would have been around to see the huge asteroid that struck Earth and caused the **extinction** of the dinosaurs.

Length: 30 feet

Height: 8 feet

Weight: 18,000 pounds

When: Late Cretaceous period—66 to 65 million years ago

Where: the forests and swamps of Montana and Wyoming in the United States, and Canada

It ate: plants

It was the size of: a school bus

It had small teeth that were shaped like a leaf.

PACHYCEPHALOSAURUS

SAY IT! PACK-ee-SEF-uh-low-SAWR-us

Pachycephalosaurus is sometimes called a "head-butting" dinosaur, but it may not have actually bumped heads with its rivals. Because the thick dome on its head was rounded, if two rivals tried to butt heads, they would have slid off each other. Some paleontologists believe that instead it may have used its dome to ram into the *side* of its rival. Whatever it was used for, the dome was over nine inches thick and made of solid bone.

It had large eyes and excellent vision.

Length: 23 feet

Height: 4 feet

Weight: 900 pounds

When: Late Cretaceous period—66 to 65 million years ago

Where: the forests of Wyoming, Montana, and South Dakota in the United States

It ate: plants

It was the size of: a car

TYRANNOSAURUS

SAY IT! Tie-RAN-oh-SAWR-us

The name *Tyrannosaurus rex* means "tyrant lizard king." Nicknamed *T. rex*, it was the largest carnivore that ever lived in North America. It had the most powerful bite of any theropod, and its teeth were strong enough to crack even the largest bones. The only thing a *T. rex* feared was another *T. rex*. Females were larger than males, probably to protect their young. But males were probably faster and more brightly colored than females. Any dinosaur that lived in the territory of a *Tyrannosaurus* had to watch out for attack.

Length: 41 feet

Height: 12 feet

Weight: 15,000 pounds

When: Late Cretaceous period—66 to 65 million years ago

Where: near forests and rivers of western North America

It ate: anything it could catch!

It was the size of: a city bus

HATZEGOPTERYX

SAY IT! hat-ze-go-OP-ter-icks

Hatzegopteryx lived at the same time as *Quetzalcoatlus*. Both pterosaurs are among the largest animals that have ever flown. Though the wingspan of *Quetzalcoatlus* is a little longer, *Hatzegopteryx*'s bones are much bigger. Unlike other giant pterosaurs, *Hatzegopteryx* has a short neck. It probably chased its prey, but what did it eat? Paleontologists think it ate dwarf dinosaurs, which lived on the same island where *Hatzegopteryx* lived. One of these dwarf dinosaurs was a sauropod called *Magyarosaurus* (maeg-yar-o-SORE-us). This long-necked, plant-eating dinosaur was about the size of a cow.

Hatzegopteryx lived on an island with no large meat-eating dinosaurs. It probably evolved to fill the important role of a predator in the ecosystem.

Wingspan: 38 feet

When: Late Cretaceous period—66 million years ago

Where: Romania

It ate: small dinosaurs

It was the size of: a giraffe

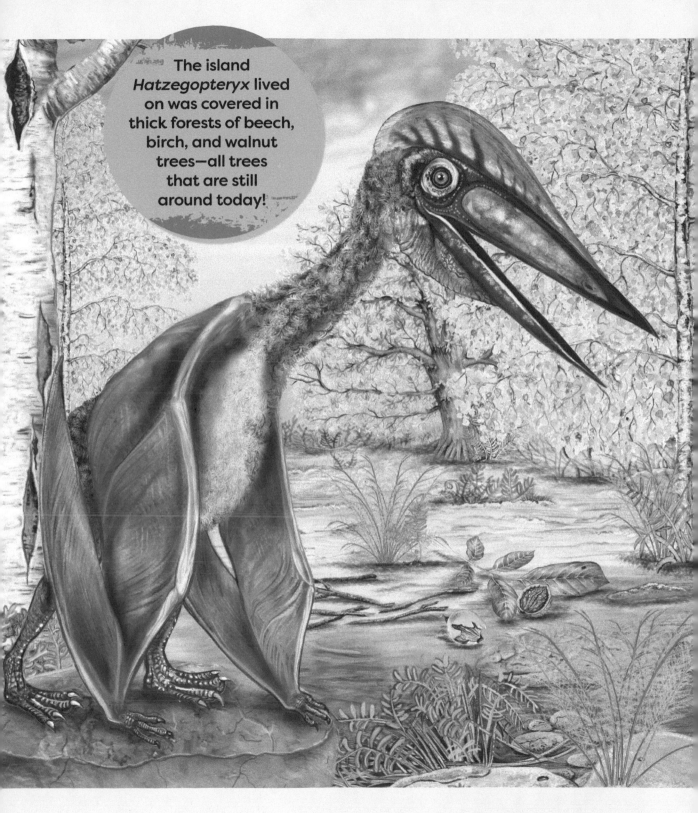

The island *Hatzegopteryx* lived on was covered in thick forests of beech, birch, and walnut trees—all trees that are still around today!

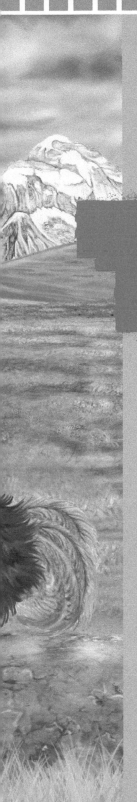

PART FOUR

CENOZOIC ERA

At the end of the Cretaceous Period, a giant asteroid struck the Earth. Most of the dinosaurs were wiped out, but some non-avian dinosaurs survived. This ended the Mesozoic Era. The Cenozoic Era began 66 million years ago and continues to this day.

ONYCHONYCTERIS

SAY IT! oh-nick-oh-NICK-tur-riss

Onychonycteris is the oldest bat fossil! Along with pterosaurs and birds, bats make up the third group of flying **vertebrates**. *Onychonycteris* looks like a normal bat, but it's also different in many ways. By observing the tiny bones inside its ears, paleontologists found that *Onychonycteris* could not **echolocate**. This is how modern bats "see" by using sound. Since *Onychonycteris* appeared on Earth only 14 million years after the dinosaurs went extinct, some of the earliest bats may have lived with dinosaurs.

Modern bats have toes that are all the same length. *Onychonycteris*'s toes were different lengths, indicating it did not hang upside down like bats do today.

Wingspan: 12 inches

When: Early Eocene epoch—52 million years ago

Where: Western United States

It ate: fruit or insects

It was the size of: a bird

EUROTROCHILUS

SAY IT! you-row-TRO-ka-luss

Unlike many of the birds in this book, *Eurotrochilus* was tiny. With a body just over an inch long, it zipped around in search of flowers. *Eurotrochilus* is the earliest-known ancestor of hummingbirds! Today, hummingbirds live in North and South America. But *Eurotrochilus* is extra special because it lived in Europe. How did a prehistoric hummingbird fly to the other side of the planet? Paleontologists don't know, but it's one more thing that makes humming-birds such amazing and fascinating birds.

All hummingbirds have specially shaped wing bones that allow them to fly forward, backward, sideways, and hover in place—they are the only birds that can do this!

Wingspan: about 2 inches

When: Early Oligocene epoch—34 to 28 million years ago

Where: France, Germany, and Poland

It ate: flower nectar

It was the size of: a mouse

DROMORNIS

SAY IT! **SAY IT! dro-MORE-niss**

Dromornis belongs to an amazing group of giant, extinct, flightless birds from Australia, commonly called the mihirungs (MEE-hee-rungs). These giant-beaked birds were closely related to ducks and geese or chickens and turkeys. *Dromornis* had big, bulky feet and powerful legs. But these legs were not built for running. *Dromornis* probably plodded along and walked everywhere. Its huge beak looks scary, but it was used to crush plant roots, big seeds, and nuts.

Height: 10 feet

Weight: 1,600 pounds

When: Late Miocene and Early Pliocene epochs—28 to 5 million years ago

Where: Australia

It ate: plants, seeds, and nuts

It was the size of: a cow

Paleontologists used to think the mihirungs were just giant, flightless geese.

PELAGORNIS

SAY IT! pa-lage-OR-niss

Pelagornis was a giant sea bird that might have been the largest flying bird ever. Even though *Pelagornis* looked like a giant albatross, it was more closely related to pelicans and storks. You might think its long beak is filled with dozens of sharp pointy "teeth," but they are not teeth! They are actually growths from the bones that make the beak. These "fake teeth" helped *Pelagornis* catch and hold on to slippery fish.

Like modern sea birds, *Pelagornis* had a large salt gland in its eye sockets. This gland helped store and get rid of extra salt from ocean water.

Wingspan: about 20 feet

When: Late Oligocene and Early Pleistocene epochs—25 to 2 million years ago

Where: United States, Chile, France, Morocco, and New Zealand

It ate: fish

Its wingspan was the size of: a giraffe

Pelagornis belongs to a group of birds often called the *pseudodontorns* (sue-dough-DON-torns), which means "the false-toothed birds."

OTODUS

SAY IT! oh-TOE-dus

Otodus was the largest predatory shark of all time. You may have heard about *Otodus* by its other name: *megalodon*. In science, plants and animals have two-part names, like *Tyrannosaurus rex*, *Boa constrictor*, or *Homo sapiens* (that's the scientific name for humans!). This ancient shark's scientific name is

Length: about 60 feet

When: Miocene to Pliocene epochs—23 to 3 million years ago

Where: North and South America, Europe, Asia, Africa, and Australia

It ate: whales, dolphins, seals, and sea turtles

It was as long as: two fire trucks end to end

Otodus megalodon. We don't normally refer to animals by the second part of their name, but this famous shark is an exception. *Otodus* was very big and had a giant appetite to match. Paleontologists have discovered several whale fossils that are covered with the bite marks from *Otodus*.

HERACLES

SAY IT! HAIR-ah-kleez

Heracles was the largest parrot of all time! The heaviest parrot alive today, the kakapo (KACK-ah-poh), weighs 9 pounds and reaches the knee of an adult. But *Heracles* would have reached an adult's waist and it weighed over 15 pounds! Paleontologists have found only two leg bones from *Heracles*, so they do not know much about this bird. But by comparing those bones to modern parrot bones, paleontologists can make scientific guesses about the size, shape, diet, and behavior of *Heracles*.

Because of its large size, paleontologists think that *Heracles* was flightless, just like the kakapo.

Wingspan: unknown

When: Early Miocene epoch—19 to 16 million years ago

Where: New Zealand

It ate: berries, fruit, and nuts

It was the size of: a large dog

Stupendemys geographicus is named in honor of the 1972 National Geographic Society expedition that found the first *Stupendemys* fossils.

STUPENDEMYS

SAY IT! stew-PEN-dem-EEZ

Stupendemys was the largest freshwater turtle. It lived in a giant wetland that covered the top half of South America. But *Stupendemys* wasn't the only giant in this ecosystem—it lived alongside the giant crocodile-like creature *Purussaurus* (pure-RAH-sawr-us) and the giant rodent *Phoberomys* (fo-BEAR-oh-meez). *Stupendemys*'s heavy shell helped it stay underwater as it slowly swam. The male had a small horn on each side of its shell. They probably used these horns to fight each other, something many turtles do today.

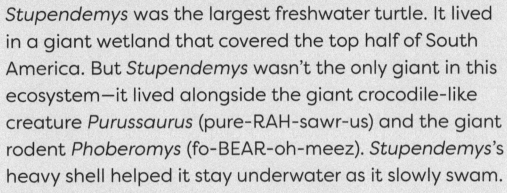

Stupendemys means "stupendous turtle," because of its giant size.

Length: 10 feet

When: Late Miocene to Early Pliocene epoch— 13 to 5 million years ago

Where: South America

It ate: fish, shellfish, and aquatic plants

Its shell was the size of: a car

ARGENTAVIS

SAY IT! ar-gin-TAY-vuss

KELENKEN

SAY IT! kell-IN-kin

Standing over 10 feet tall, *Kelenken* was a top predator with a large, powerful beak. But *Kelenken* didn't fly to catch unsuspecting prey—it ran after its prey. While *Kelenken* ran on the ground, the giant *Argentavis* soared in the skies above. Riding on air currents like modern condors and vultures, *Argentavis* likely patrolled the skies for prey. Its large beak and claws could have been used for catching prey, but paleontologists think that *Argentavis* probably fed on already-dead animals.

Wingspan: 21 feet

When: Late Miocene epoch—9 to 6 million years ago

Where: Argentina

It ate: dead animals

It was the size of: a killer whale

Wingspan: unknown

When: Middle Miocene epoch—15 million years ago

Where: Argentina

It ate: large rodents, snakes, and deerlike animals

It was as tall as: an elephant

Livyatan's species name is *melvillei*, in honor of the author Herman Melville. His famous book *Moby-Dick* is about a large, white sperm whale that attacks ships.

LIVYATAN

SAY IT! la-VIE-uh-tan

With a 10-foot-long skull, *Livyatan* is the largest whale with teeth ever discovered. Its huge, banana-size teeth were on its upper and lower jaws. *Livyatan* is related to the modern sperm whale. Today, the sperm whale dives deep in the ocean to hunt giant squids. But paleontologists think that *Livyatan* probably hunted other whales near the water's surface. *Livyatan* also lived alongside the giant shark *Otodus megalodon*. Did *Livyatan* and *Otodus* compete for food? It is fascinating to wonder how two giant predators lived together in the same ecosystem.

The name *Livyatan* refers to the biblical monster Leviathan.

Length: up to 57 feet

When: Miocene period—9 to 8 million years ago

Where: South America

It ate: other whales and marine vertebrates

It was as long as: a semitruck

VOROMBE

Vorombe belongs to a group of big, flightless birds called "elephant birds." Almost 10 feet tall, *Vorombe* was estimated to weigh 1,900 pounds, making it the heaviest bird of all time! It had tiny wings and walked around on powerful legs. Paleontologists think that it had a good sense of smell and was active at night. You might think that elephant birds were related to today's ostriches or emus, but they're not! Their closest relative is the small, flightless, **nocturnal** kiwi from New Zealand.

Wingspan: unknown

When: Pleistocene and Holocene epochs—2 million to 1,000 years ago

Where: Madagascar

It ate: fruit, seeds, and nuts

It was as tall as: a basketball hoop

The elephant birds went extinct about 1,000 years ago.

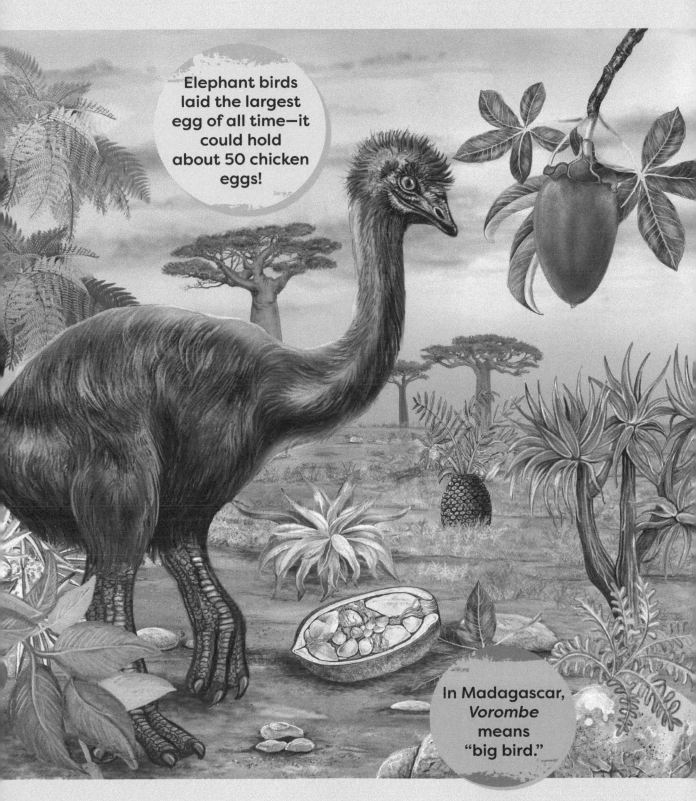

HIERAAETUS

SAY IT! hi-RAH-ah-tuss

Hieraaetus, also known as the Haast's eagle, is the largest eagle that ever lived. With a wingspan of nearly 10 feet and weighing over 30 pounds, *Hieraaetus* soared above the forests and grasslands of New Zealand. *Hieraaetus* had claws that were 3 inches long. It was the top predator in its ecosystem and preyed on the *moa* (MO-ah), which were large, flightless birds similar to the elephant birds. Several *moa* fossils show broken bones caused by *Hieraaetus*'s talons and beak.

Hieraaetus lived on Earth so recently that the native people of New Zealand, the Māori, have folktales about living alongside it.

Wingspan: almost 10 feet

When: Pleistocene and Holocene epochs— 2.5 million to 500 years ago

Where: New Zealand

It ate: meat

It was the size of: an eagle

GLOSSARY

ambush: To hide and then attack by surprise

anatomist: A scientist who studies the structure of bodies

ankylosaurs: Plant-eating dinosaurs that had protective body armor, horns, and spikes. Some had clubs on their tails.

aquatic: Living in water

armor: Hard protection on the outside of an animal's body. Just like knights wear suits of armor to protect themselves, many animals evolved bony coverings for protection.

asteroid: A piece of rock that floats in space and orbits the sun

carnivore: An animal that eats only meat

cartilage: Tissue that makes up a human nose and ears. Cartilage is softer and more flexible than keratin or bone, but still provides support and shape for body parts.

ceratopsians: Four-legged, plant-eating dinosaurs with sharp beaks, horns, and frills

conifer: A tall, thin tree with sharp needles instead of leaves. Also called pine trees.

convergent evolution: When plants or animals look similar but are not related. For example, a shark and a dolphin are similarly shaped because they both swim in the ocean, not because they are closely related.

crest: A tuft of feathers, bone, or skin on the head of an animal

dromaeosaurs: Also called raptors, these are meat-eating dinosaurs with curved claws on their feet

echolocate: "See" with sound. Animals like bats, whales, and dolphins make high-pitched sounds that create a picture of what's around them.

ecosystem: A community of plants, animals, and their environment

evolution: The way all plants and animals change over time. Through multiple generations, small changes add up and cause a new species to be different from the old one.

evolved: To have changed over time, starting with something simple and changing into something more complex

extinct: Having died out and completely disappeared, as with plants and animals that used to live on Earth

extinction: The death of an entire species, or group, of animals

fossil: A plant or animal that has slowly been turned to stone by minerals in the ground

fossilization: The process of turning a plant or animal into stone

frill: A bony plate surrounding a dinosaur's skull

gastric pellets: Parts of a bird's food that they spit out rather than digest

gastroliths: Rocks that are swallowed whole and then roll around in the stomach to grind up food

gill rakers: Small pieces of bone in the back of some fish mouths

graveyard: A location where more than one dinosaur skeleton has been found

herbivore: An animal that only eats plants

iridescent: Shiny and appearing like different colors from different angles

keratin: A type of protein that makes up hair and fingernails

marine: Living in the ocean

marsupial: Order of mammals that include kangaroos, koalas, and possums

mate: A dinosaur of the opposite sex that becomes the parent of offspring

melanosomes: The part of a cell that stores color

migrate: To move from one place to another, usually in search of food or water

nocturnal: Awake and active at night

omnivore: An animal that eats both plants and meat

ornithopods: Plant-eating dinosaurs with birdlike feet and beaks, some of which looked like duck bills

osteoderms: Pieces of thick bone material attached to the outside of the skin that are used like body armor to protect the dinosaur from attack

pachycephalosaurs: Two-legged dinosaurs with domes or armored skulls that ate plants

pack: A group of three or more of the same species of meat-eating dinosaurs that work together to hunt for food

paleontologist: A scientist who digs up and studies the remains of plants and animals of the past

predator: Meat-eating animals that hunt living animals for food

prehistoric: The time before written history

prey: The food source of a meat eater or something that is hunted by others

pterosaurs: Flying reptiles that lived at the same time as the dinosaurs. They were not dinosaurs, but close relatives.

pycnofibers: Hairlike fibers on pterosaurs. Pycnofibers are not hair, but they are very similar. They probably helped keep pterosaurs warm, just like hair helps keep mammals warm.

raptors: Common name for dromaeosaurs

sauropod: Dinosaurs with long necks and tails. They stood on four legs and ate only plants.

sauropodomorphs: The long-necked plant eaters, which include the sauropods

scavenger: An animal that eats things that were already dead

scientific name: The name that scientists use for a plant or animal. Scientific names have two parts: the first name is for the group that the plant or animal belongs to, and the second name identifies the particular species.

serrated: Covered with sharp, jagged points that help slice through meat

species: A group of animals that are closely related

specimen: An individual animal, fossil, or skeleton

stegosaurs: Four-legged plant eaters that had plates on their backs and spikes on their tails

territory: The area or location that is claimed by a meat-eating dinosaur to be its own property

theropods: Meat-eating dinosaurs that walked on two legs

transitional fossil: A fossil that has traits common to both creatures that lived before it and creatures that lived after it

vegetation: Different types of plants that live in the same area

vertebrate: Any animal with a skeleton made up of bones or cartilage

wingspan: The distance that a creature's wings stretch, from tip to tip

INDEX

ABOUT THE AUTHORS

"DINOSAUR GEORGE" BLASING has studied and excavated dinosaurs and other prehistoric life for more than 35 years. He is a public speaker, author, and television writer. He also owns a traveling dinosaur museum that brings the prehistoric world to young people and adults across the country.

In 2007, he co-created, wrote, and hosted a 12-part television series for the History Channel called *Jurassic Fight Club*. The series was shown in more than 25 countries and seen by over 30 million viewers. Although he enjoyed working for the History Channel, his true passion is teaching children. Since 1997, Dinosaur George has performed live to over 4 million students and adults throughout the United States and Canada, and has appeared at over 5,000 schools, museums, and public events.

Dinosaur George is also an animal behaviorist, studying modern animals and comparing their behavior to animals of the past. In his spare time, he hosts a podcast and runs social media pages dedicated to children.

He was born in Colorado but moved to Texas at an early age. He grew up on a farm near San Antonio and loves the outdoors. When he's not digging up dinosaurs, hosting a podcast, or traveling with his museum, Dinosaur George enjoys camping, hiking, and being outdoors with nature. Visit him online at DinosaurGeorge.com.

CARY WOODRUFF grew up in rural Central Virginia and received his bachelor's and master's degrees at Montana State University under famed dinosaur paleontologist Dr. Jack Horner. Currently, Cary is the director of paleontology at the Great Plains Dinosaur Museum in Malta, Montana. He is also a doctoral student at the University of Toronto under Dr. David Evans. Cary specializes in sauropod dinosaurs. His pioneering studies on sauropod growth are changing our understanding of the lives of the biggest animals to ever walk on Earth. Cary has also published research on the first burrowing dinosaur, modern cow vertebral anatomy, dinosaur vision, stegosaurs, and fossil manatees in ancient Egyptian catacombs.

ABOUT THE ILLUSTRATORS

ANNALISA AND MARINA DURANTE are nature and science illustrators. They are twin sisters who have loved nature and animals since they were children. Marina enjoys hiking, deep-water diving, and photography. The photos she takes while exploring nature are the inspiration for her art. Annalisa is inspired by Eastern philosophy and enjoys meditating as she explores the outdoors.

In 2001, Marina and Annalisa were invited by the Galapagos National Park to draw the birds of the Galapagos Islands. They have worked for the Food and Agriculture Organization of the United Nations, illustrating recently discovered species of fish. Their works have been published all over the world, and they have won a number of international art prizes. They especially enjoy illustrating portraits of animals and pets. Find them online at DuranteIllustrations.com.

CPSIA information can be obtained
at www.ICGtesting.com
Printed in the USA
JSHW011502291221
21557JS00006B/6